the
concise illustrator's
reference manual
figures

BLOOMSBURY

A QUARTO BOOK

Copyright © 1995 Quarto Publishing plc

First published in 1995 by
Bloomsbury Publishing plc
2 Soho Square
London W1V 6HB

A CIP catalogue record of this book is available from the British Library.

ISBN 0-7475-2307-X

This book was designed and produced by
Quarto Publishing plc
The Old Brewery, 6 Blundell Street
London N7 9BH

Photographers: Mick Dunn & Dick Hatfield
Designer: Neal Cobourne
Assistant Editor: Peg Osterman

Printed in Hong Kong by Regent Publishing Services Limited

CONTENTS

LAW AND ORDER
4.01 New York policeman - stop!
4.02 New York policeman directing traffic
4.03 Saluting
4.04 Gangster with violin case

THE WORKING DAY
5.01 Hailing a taxi
5.02 Running and looking at watch
5.03 Opening an umbrella
5.04 Standing under an umbrella
5.05 Taking dictation
5.06 Commuting
5.07 Heavy suitcase
5.08 On the phone
5.09 Typing

CARRYING
6.01 Stack of boxes
6.02 Large plant
6.03 Step ladder
6.04 Smelly socks

DOMESTIC
7.01 Painting with a roller
7.02 Leaning on a broom
7.03 Sawing
7.04 Hammering
7.05 Painting with a brush

EATING AND DRINKING
8.01 Eating sandwiches and drinking tea
8.02 Drinking from a teacup and saucer
8.03 Priest with tea and biscuits
8.04 Waitress with tray

MUSIC AND ENTERTAINMENT
9.01 Rock and roll dancing
9.02 Ballroom dancing - quickstep
9.03 Ballroom dancing - waltz
9.04 Ballroom dancing - tango
9.05 Disco dancing
9.06 Conducting - vivace
9.07 Conducting - adagio
9.08 Playing the clarinet
9.09 Playing the double bass
9.10 Playing the violin
9.11 Opera singer
9.12 Rock singer
9.13 Playing the acoustic guitar
9.14 Playing the electric guitar
9.15 Playing the keyboard
9.16 Jazz trumpeter

DRESSING
10.01 Putting on a hat
10.02 Putting on a jacket
10.03 Putting on trousers
10.04 Putting on socks
10.05 Putting on shoes
10.06 Taking off boots
10.07 Drying hair

PIN-UPS
11.01 Pin-up
11.02 Pin-up
11.03 Pin-up
11.04 Pin-up
11.05 Pin-up
11.06 Pin-up
11.07 Pin-up
11.08 Pin-up

USING THE FIGURE REFERENCE MANUAL

This manual comprises 122 "poses" categorized under 11 general headings. Each category has an index code, and within each category each pose has a further sub-index code for ease of reference.

Waist-level camera angle

Each pose is presented from six angles. The images are as large as the pose will conveniently allow. A consistent scale is maintained within the camera angles on each pose, but the scale may change from one pose to another.

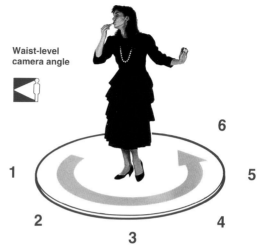

Each pose is presented from six angles, achieved by using a waist-level camera and a turntable rotated through 360 degrees

Category heading

Pose title

ND ENTERTAINMENT

keyboard 9·15

Index and sub-index code

Composite figures can be drawn using elements from different poses.

Pose A

Pose B

Pose C

Composite pose

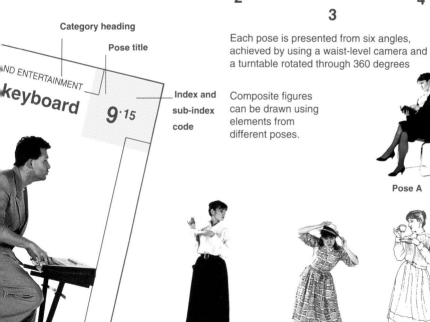

1·01 Skiing - schuss

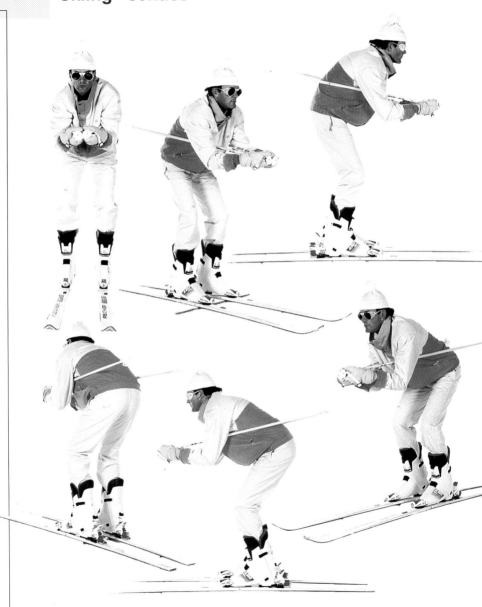

Skier - carrying skis

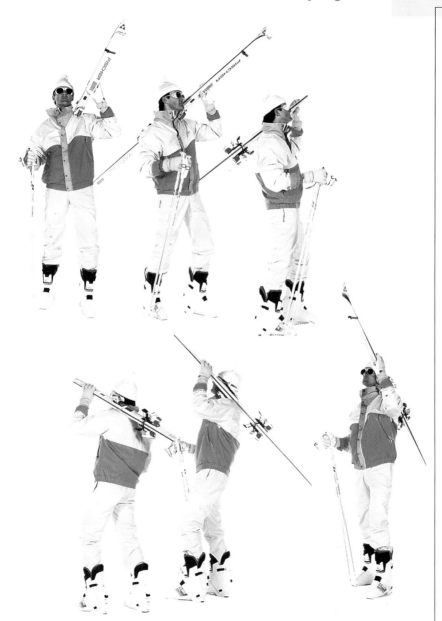

1·03   Skiing - admiring the view

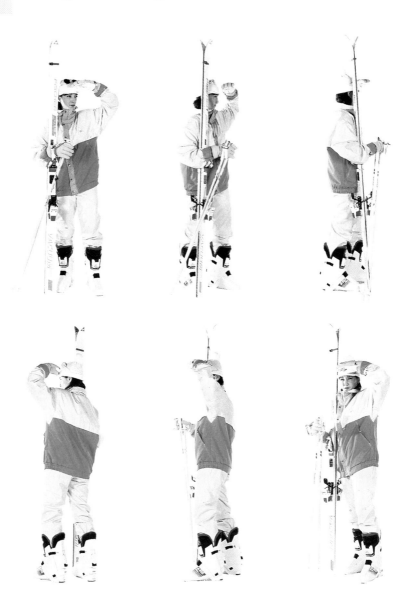

Golf - admiring the shot

1·05 Golf - addressing the ball

Golf - backswing

1·07 Tennis - ready to receive

Tennis - forehand drive

1·09 Badminton - smash

Squash - forehand 1·10

1.11   Squash - backhand

Cricket - defensive block

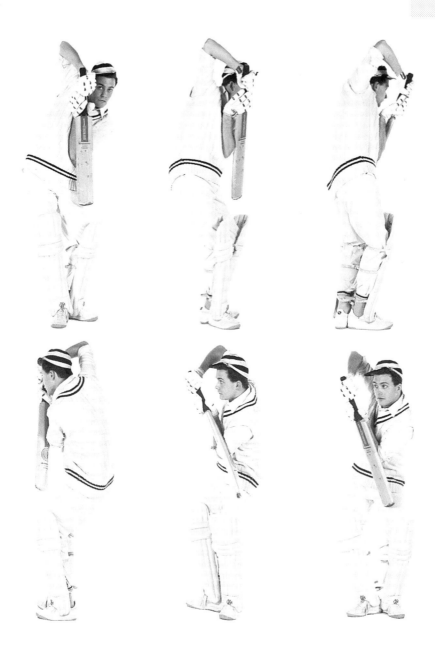

1·13 Cricket - waiting to bat

Throwing a ball

1·15 Tossing up a ball

1·17 Bowling

Soccer - throw-in

1·19 Running - sprinter on the block

Rugby - passing

1·21 Rugby - drop kick

Basketball - dribbling 1·22

1·23 Basketball - shooting

Boxing - classic guard

1·25 Boxing - jabbing

1·27 Weightlifting - one-arm dumbbell

1·29 Skipping rope

Gymnastics 1·30

1·31 Gymnastics - headstand

1·33 Exercising - toe touch

Exercising - end of the workout

1·35 **Exercising - stretching**

1·37 Yoga

1·39 Skateboarding

1·41 Walking with stick

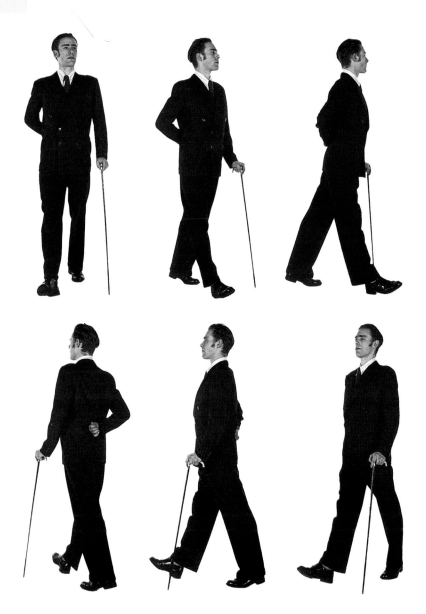

Playing cards 1·42

1·43 Artist painting

In a chair doing the crossword

In a chair looking through an address book

2·04   Sideways in a chair

Kneeling on a chair and talking on the phone

2·06   On a bar stool

Priest asleep in a rocking chair

2·08 On the floor thinking

3·01 Couple kissing

3·03   # Crying into handkerchief

3·05 GI greeting his girl

3^{·07} **Couple sitting**

Couple sitting at a table

3·09   Bully threatening someone

3·11 Taking the lady home

Couple at the beach 3·12

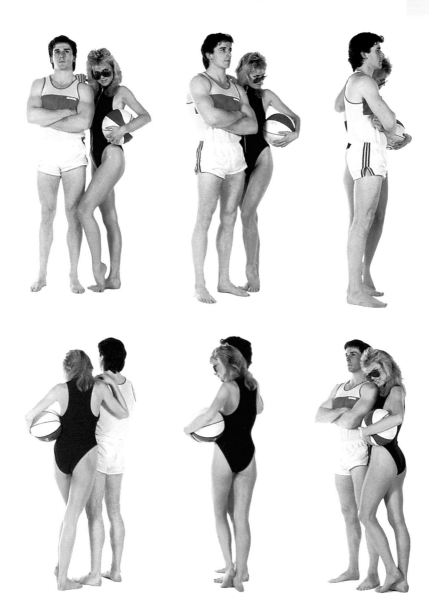

3·13 **Praying**

4·02 New York policeman directing traffic

Saluting 4·03

4·04 Gangster with violin case

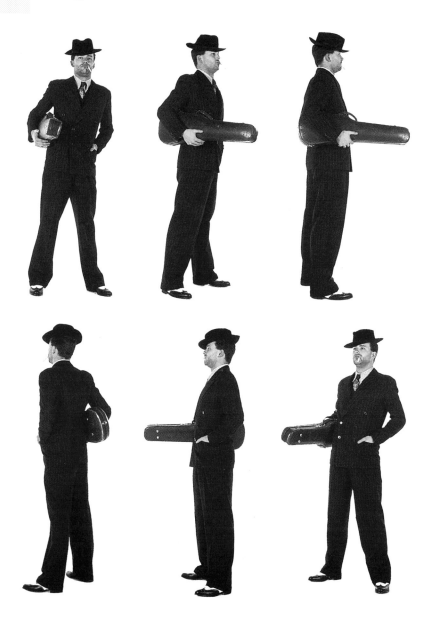

Hailing a taxi

5·02 Running and looking at watch

5·04 Standing under an umbrella

5·06 Commuting

5·08 On the phone

6·01 **Stack of boxes**

6·03 Step ladder

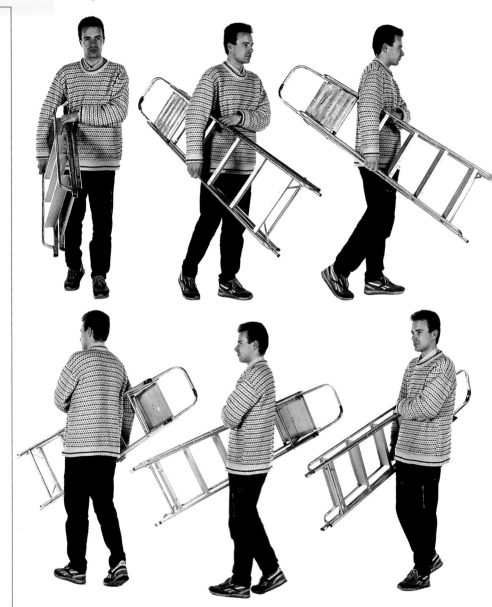

7.01 Painting with a roller

Leaning on a broom

7·03 Sawing

7·05 Painting with a brush

Eating sandwiches and drinking tea   8·01

8·02 Drinking from a teacup and saucer

Priest with tea and biscuits

8·04 Waitress with tray

Ballroom dancing - quickstep

Ballroom dancing - waltz **9**·03

9·04 Ballroom dancing - tango

9·06 Conducting - vivace

9·08 Playing the clarinet

9·10 Playing the violin

9·12 Rock singer

9·14 Playing the electric guitar

Jazz trumpeter

10·02 Putting on a jacket

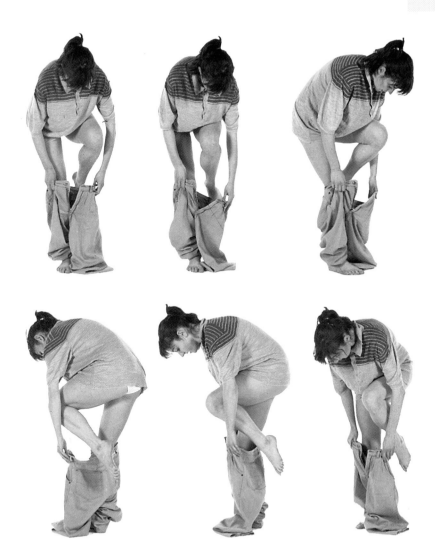

10·04 Putting on socks

10·06 Taking off boots

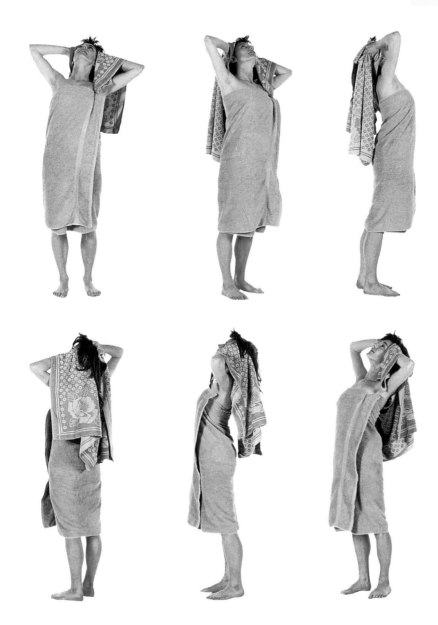

11·01 Pin-up

Pin-up

Pin-up

11·07 Pin-up

ACKNOWLEDGMENTS

Quarto Publishing would like to thank the following for their
assistance in the production of this book:

Alpine Sports Ltd
Bapty & Co. Ltd (weapons & militaria)
Estia Designs Ltd
Gordon Grose Sports
Lonsdale Sports Equipment Ltd
Mardi Gras (costumiers)
20th Century Props (costumiers)
Lee Robinson
Ben Smithies
Lousie Talbot-Weiss

CREDITS

Quarto Publishing would like to thank the following actors,
actresses and models for their work on this book:

Steve Beresford
Orla Brady
Matt Burton
Lucinda Galloway
Ruth Gordon
Simon Lambert
James Lumsden
Hannah Orthmann
John Sinnott
Carmen Stipetic